# IF THE DINOSAURS COULD TALK...

## *PLESIOSAURUS*

### Stuart A. Kallen

ILLUSTRATED
BY
KRISTEN COPHAM

Published by Abdo & Daughters, 4940 Viking Drive, Suite 622, Edina, Minnesota 55435.

Library bound edition distributed by Rockbottom Books, Pentagon Tower, P.O. Box 36036, Minneapolis, Minnesota 55435.

Printed in the United States.

**Illustrations by Kristen Copham**


## Edited By Julie Berg


### LIBRARY OF CONGRESS CATALOGING-IN-PUBLICATION DATA

Kallen, Stuart A., 1955—
    Plesiosaurus / Stuart A. Kallen ; [edited by Julie Berg].
        p. cm. -- (If the Dinosaurs could Talk--)
    ISBN 1-56239-287-5
    1. Plesiosaurus -- Juvenile literature. [1. Plesiosaurus. 2. Dinosaurs.]
    I. Berg, Julie. II. Title. III. Series: Kallen, Stuart A., 1955—
    If the Dinosaurs could Talk.
    QE862.P4K35       1994
    567.9'7 -- dc20
                                   94-6356
                                   CIP
                                   AC

What's that green thing bobbing in the sea?

Is it an island?

Is it a giant tree?

Look closer! It's a real, live sea serpent. And it's swimming over here to tell you a story— a story about the time when monster reptiles ruled the ocean waves.

Ahoy there friend! I'm a *Plesiosaurus*. That's a big word to chew on. But say it like five words. Then it's easy. Try it! Plees. Ee. Uh. SAWR. Us. *Plesiosaurus!* That's a pleasing name.

I lived in the warm oceans 100 million years ago. Some may call me a dinosaur of the deep. But I'm not really a dino. I'm a reptile — like a turtle, snake, or lizard. My name means "near lizard." But I'm no lizard.

I do *look* like a dinosaur. I'm more than 10 feet long. But I have flippers instead of feet. I'm a strong swimmer. I move my flippers like a bird flaps its wings.

**That's how I swim through the water with the greatest of ease.**

Once upon a time, *Plesiosaurs* lived on land. But there wasn't enough food for us to eat. So we went to live in the sea where there were plenty of fish to munch on. After millions of years, our feet changed into fins for swimming. And our necks became very long.

My head hovers above the water looking for fish to eat. When I see one, I plunge down and grab it in my powerful jaws.

No slippery fish can wiggle out of my sharp teeth.

The seas I live in are full of monster swimming reptiles.

My cousin is called *Elasmosaurus* (ee-lass-mo-SAWR-us). That critter is 50 feet long. And its neck is half as long as its body! With a neck that long, it can strike like lightning at passing fish.

One scientist said that the *Elasmosaurus* looks like "a snake strung through the body of a turtle."

Scientists did not know about monster sea reptiles until the year 1813. That's when 13-year-old Mary Anning found *Plesiosaurus* bones in England. Mary was digging for fossils. She saw some bones sticking out of a cliff. She got a hammer and chisel and dug out the skeleton of a *Plesiosaurus!*

*Plesiosaurs* became extinct about 70 million years ago. But we live on in myth and legend. For years people have been talking about the Loch Ness Monster. That beast, named "Nessie", is supposed to live in a lake in Scotland. People claim to have seen Nessie. There are even a few blurry photos. So far, no one has been able to prove if Nessie is real.

But everyone says she looks just like me!

Well, I hope you had a pleasing time talking to a *Plesiosaurus*. I know I had fun talking to you. But it's time for me to go fishing. This serpent's got to surf. Bye, bye!

# GLOSSARY

**Elasmosaurus** - a 50-foot swimming reptile, now extinct.

**Extinct** - no longer in living form.

**Fin** - a thin, flat projection from the body of a fish, used to propel or steer the fish through the water.

**Flipper** - a limb of certain sea animals used in swimming.

**Fossils** - the remains of a prehistoric animal or plant buried in the earth and hardened like rock.

**Legend** - a story handed down from the past.

**Myth** - a traditional story containing ideas or beliefs about ancient times.

**Plesiosaurus** - an extinct reptile that swam the oceans millions of years ago.

**Reptile** - a cold-blooded animal with a backbone and fairly short legs.

**Serpent** - a snake.